THE LIFE OF JESUS

An Illustrated Rosary

Mary Billingsley

Foreword by
Fr. Benedict J. Groeschel, C.F.R.

Eerdmans Books for Young Readers

Grand Rapids, Michigan • Cambridge, U.K.

This book is dedicated to Mary Mother of God.
— *M.B.*

I wish to thank my husband, John Matt, for his excellent opinions, his encouragement, and his loving support throughout this creative effort. I also appreciate his constant patience and readiness to help whenever I needed computer assistance.

In addition, my son, Andrew Matt, deserves many, many thanks for his meticulous proofreading of the text. His positive attitude and helpful suggestions are also deeply appreciated.

Text and illustrations © 2010 Mary Billingsley

Published in 2010 by Eerdmans Books for Young Readers
an imprint of Wm. B. Eerdmans Publishing Co.

Wm. B. Eerdmans Publishing Co.
2140 Oak Industrial Dr. NE, Grand Rapids, Michigan 49505
P.O. Box 163, Cambridge CB3 9PU U.K.

www.eerdmans.com/youngreaders

Manufactured at Tien Wah Press in Singapore, October 2009; first printing

10 11 12 13 14 15 16   9 8 7 6 5 4 3 2 1

Library of Congress Cataloging-in-Publication Data

Billingsley, Mary, 1938-
The life of Jesus : paintings and meditations on the Rosary / written and illustrated by Mary Billingsley.
p. cm.
ISBN 978-0-8028-5362-2 (alk. paper)
1. Rosary--Juvenile literature. I. Title.
BX2163.B46 2010
242'.74--dc22
2009026237

CONTENTS

FOREWORD

This exquisitely beautiful book by Mary Billingsley presents the rosary for children, but I might add — for children of all ages. When I first saw a few of the paintings, I wondered if it was wise to portray Christ, Our Lady, and the other participants in the drama of the rosary as puppets or manikin figures. But the idea very much grew on me, and as I now see the final outcome of Mary's work, I'm completely captivated. This is a rosary book for young and old.

Quite beyond the fact that children will find it attractive and will be able to deal with the figures of the rosary as they are presented, there is another far deeper meaning to all of this, and this is where the older grown-up children like us may be able to learn something too.

What is it we can learn? That our world looks to the transcendent and infinite God much like the world of puppets looks to human beings. We take ourselves terribly seriously as human beings. But remember that the Incarnate Word had to empty himself, taking on the form of a slave in order to save us. Mary's sensitive presentation of the rosary in these figures that are meant for children provides a good deal of visual meditation for anyone. These figures are filled with beauty, gentleness, pathos, and hope. Often when I'm preaching at an important event I preach to the children who are there and let the adults listen. You can often say to children in very simple ways what adults need to hear but can understand better when presented in the direct way that you speak to children.

The use of the words of the Bible is very helpful and important. I would suggest to any adult looking at these pictures to read them through a couple of times. You will be changed in some of your meditations and thoughts. And isn't this what prayer is about? It is meant to change us, and in that respect Mary Billingsley has made a very real contribution to Catholic spiritual art, which is intended to raise the heart and mind to God. If I may humbly say so, I think Our Blessed Lady, who almost always appeared to children, will be pleased with this work of art in her honor.

— *Fr. Benedict J. Groeschel, C.F.R.*

An internationally known lecturer and retreat master, Father Benedict J. Groeschel, C.F.R., is professor of pastoral psychology at St. Joseph's Seminary in Yonkers, New York. The director of the Office for Spiritual Development of the Archdiocese of New York, he is also a founding member of the Franciscan Friars of the Renewal. A prolific author and regular guest on EWTN, Father Benedict is the founder of Trinity Retreat, a center of prayer and study for the clergy in Larchmont, New York.

The Prayers of the Rosary

The Sign of the Cross

In the name of the Father, and of the Son, and of the Holy Spirit.
Amen.

The Apostles' Creed

I believe in God, the Father Almighty, Creator of heaven and earth; and in Jesus
Christ, his only Son, our Lord, who was conceived by the Holy Spirit, born of the
Virgin Mary, suffered under Pontius Pilate, was crucified, died, and was buried. He
descended into hell; the third day he rose again from the dead. He ascended into
heaven, and is seated at the right hand of God, the Father Almighty. From thence
he shall come to judge the living and the dead. I believe in the Holy Spirit, the Holy
Catholic Church, the communion of saints, the forgiveness of sins, the resurrection
of the body, and life everlasting.

Amen.

Our Father

Our Father who art in heaven, hallowed be thy name. Thy kingdom come, thy will be
done on earth as it is in heaven. Give us this day our daily bread, and forgive us our
trespasses, as we forgive those who trespass against us, and lead us not into temptation,
but deliver us from evil.

Amen.

Hail Mary

Hail Mary, full of grace, the Lord is with thee. Blessed art thou among women, and
blessed is the fruit of thy womb, Jesus. Holy Mary, Mother of God, pray for us sinners,
now and at the hour of our death.

Amen.

Glory Be

Glory be to the Father, and to the Son, and to the Holy Spirit. As it was in the beginning,
is now, and ever shall be, world without end.

Amen.

THE FIVE JOYFUL MYSTERIES

Hail Mary full of Grace, the Lord is with Thee.
Blessed art thou among women,
and blessed is the fruit of thy womb, Jesus.
Holy Mary, Mother of God, pray for us sinners,
now and at the hour of our death. Amen.

The Annunciation
The First Joyful Mystery

Our Father

The angel Gabriel was sent by God to a poor Jewish girl
living in a little village called Nazareth. Her name was Mary.
Hail Mary

She was in her simple home one day when the angel appeared and said,
"Hail Mary, full of grace, the Lord is with thee."
Hail Mary

She was very surprised by these words and wondered what this greeting could mean.
Hail Mary

But the angel said to her, "Mary, do not be afraid, because you are special in God's eyes."
Hail Mary

"Listen! You are to have a baby, God's son, and you must name him Jesus."
Hail Mary

"Jesus will be great and will be called Son of the Most High,
and his kingdom will last forever."
Hail Mary

Mary said to the angel, "But how can this happen, since I am a virgin?"
Hail Mary

The angel answered, "The Holy Spirit will come and will cover you with his shadow."
Hail Mary

"And so the baby will be holy and will be called the Son of God."
Hail Mary

"I am the servant of the Lord," said Mary.
"Let what you have said be done to me."
Hail Mary

Glory be to the Father, and to the Son, and to the Holy Spirit.
As it was in the beginning, is now, and ever shall be, world without end.
Amen.

THE VISITATION
The Second Joyful Mystery

Our Father

The angel had told Mary that her cousin Elizabeth, an old woman, was also going to have a baby. Zechariah was her husband. Mary quickly set out on a long journey to the hill country to help her cousin.
Hail Mary

Now as soon as she heard Mary's greeting, Elizabeth was filled with the Holy Spirit, and the baby in her womb leaped for joy. She said, "Who am I that the mother of my Lord should come to me?"
Hail Mary

She then said to Mary with a loud cry,
"Of all women you are the most blessed, and blessed is the fruit of your womb."
Hail Mary

"Yes, blessed is she who believed that the promise made to her by God would come true."
Hail Mary

And Mary said to Elizabeth, "My being proclaims the greatness of the Lord,
and my spirit finds joy in God my Savior, for he has looked upon his servant in her lowliness."
Hail Mary

"All ages to come shall call me blessed.
God who is mighty has done great things for me. Holy is his name."
Hail Mary

"He has shown his power by pulling down the proud princes from their thrones
and lifting up the poor and lonely."
Hail Mary

"He fills the hungry with good things to eat
and sends away the rich who do not share."
Hail Mary

Earlier Zechariah had been told by the angel Gabriel that
God would perform a miracle: his wife, Elizabeth, would have a baby.
Hail Mary

Because he did not trust the angel's word,
he was not able to speak until the day the baby was born. The baby was named John.
Hail Mary

Glory be to the Father, and to the Son, and to the Holy Spirit.
As it was in the beginning, is now, and ever shall be, world without end.
Amen.

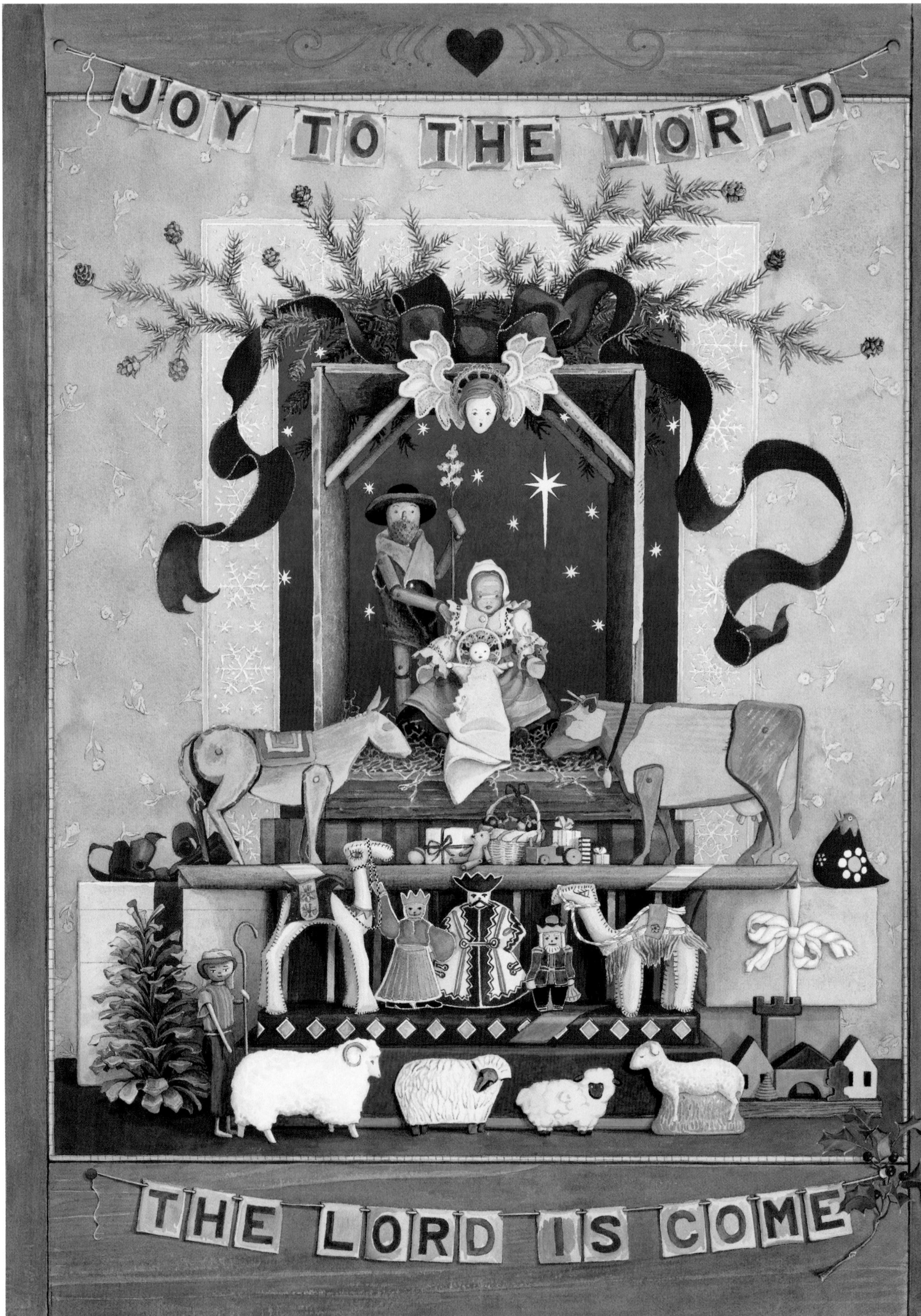
JOY TO THE WORLD
THE LORD IS COME

The Nativity
The Third Joyful Mystery

Our Father

God chose a good man named Joseph to be Mary's husband and the earthly father of Jesus.
Hail Mary

They went to Bethlehem because all the people were asked by the Roman governor
to return to their hometowns to be counted.
Hail Mary

The little town of Bethlehem was full of people, and there was no place for them to stay at an inn.
Hail Mary

Joseph found a stable under the stars. Jesus was born that night among the animals.
Mary carefully wrapped him in a soft blanket and laid him on a bed of straw in a manger.
Hail Mary

In the countryside nearby, shepherds were watching over their sheep
when suddenly an angel appeared to them.
Hail Mary

The angel said, "Behold, I bring you good news of great joy!
Today in the town of David a Savior has been born to you.
He is Christ the Lord. You will find him lying in a manger."
Hail Mary

A choir of angels in heaven sang,
"Glory to God in the highest and peace to all men of goodwill."
Hail Mary

Full of wonder, the shepherds hurried to adore Baby Jesus,
bringing him their simple food and playing music on their handmade flutes.
Hail Mary

Later, three wise men from faraway places followed a great star to find the Christ Child.
They brought wonderful gifts of gold, frankincense, and myrrh — gifts for a king.
Hail Mary

Mary and Joseph were amazed.
Mary watched all these things that were happening and remembered them in her heart.
Hail Mary

Glory be to the Father, and to the Son, and to the Holy Spirit.
As it was in the beginning, is now, and ever shall be, world without end.
Amen.

Presentation in the Temple
The Fourth Joyful Mystery

Our Father

Joseph and Mary brought their baby, Jesus, to the temple to present him to the Lord.
Joseph carried the offering of two white doves.
Hail Mary

Old Simeon, a holy and honorable man, met them in the temple.
The Holy Spirit had promised Simeon that he would not die until he had seen the Messiah.
Hail Mary

When he received the baby from Mary, Simeon immediately recognized the child
as the one he had been waiting for all those long years.
Hail Mary

Simeon said, "Now, Master, you can dismiss your servant in peace.
You have fulfilled your word, because my eyes have seen the Savior of the world."
Hail Mary

He said to Mary, "This child is destined to be the downfall and the rise of many in Israel,
a sign that will be opposed."
Hail Mary

He also said to her, "And a sword will pierce your soul too,
so that the secret thoughts of many may be laid bare."
Hail Mary

Mary listened to these serious words and kept them in her heart.
Hail Mary

Just then, old Anna, a holy woman who was always praying in the temple,
came upon this scene and also recognized the Messiah.
Hail Mary

The Holy Spirit watched over from above.
Hail Mary

The Holy Family went back to Nazareth.
Baby Jesus grew up and was filled with wisdom, and God's favor was with him.
Hail Mary

Glory be to the Father, and to the Son, and to the Holy Spirit.
As it was in the beginning, is now, and ever shall be, world without end.
Amen.

Son why have you done this to us? You see that your father and I have been searching for you in sorrow

Why did you search for me? Did you not know that I must be in my father's house?

Finding Jesus in the Temple
The Fifth Joyful Mystery

Our Father

When Jesus was twelve years old,
the Holy Family went up to Jerusalem for the feast of Passover.
Hail Mary

When they were returning home,
the boy Jesus stayed behind in Jerusalem without his parents knowing it.
Hail Mary

Joseph, the protector of the Holy Family,
took Mary back to Jerusalem, where they looked for Jesus everywhere.
Three days later, they found him in the temple.
Hail Mary

Jesus was sitting in the middle of the teachers,
listening to them and asking them questions.
Hail Mary

All those who heard him were amazed at his intelligence and his answers.
Hail Mary

Mary said to Jesus, "Son, why have you done this to us?
You see that your father and I have been searching for you in sorrow."
Hail Mary

Jesus answered, "Why did you search for me?
Did you not know that I must be in my Father's house?"
Hail Mary

But they did not know what he meant.
Hail Mary

He obediently left the teachers and joined Mary and Joseph and returned to Nazareth,
where he grew in wisdom and age and grace before God and men.
Hail Mary

His mother treasured all these things in her heart.
Hail Mary

Glory be to the Father, and to the Son, and to the Holy Spirit.
As it was in the beginning, is now, and ever shall be, world without end.
Amen.

THE FIVE LUMINOUS MYSTERIES

Baptism of Jesus
The First Luminous Mystery

Our Father

In those days John the Baptist, the son of Elizabeth and Zechariah,
was preaching in the wilderness, "Repent, for the kingdom of heaven is at hand."
Hail Mary

The prophet Isaiah had spoken of John when he said, "The voice of one crying in the wilderness:
Prepare the way of the Lord, make his paths straight."
Hail Mary

John was clothed in camel's hair, wore a leather belt around his waist,
and ate locusts and wild honey.
Hail Mary

Many people came to confess their sins and be baptized by John in the river Jordan.
Hail Mary

John told the people, "I baptize you with water for repentance,
but he who is coming after me is mightier than I; I am not worthy to unfasten his sandals.
He will baptize you with the Holy Spirit."
Hail Mary

Then Jesus, a grown man, came up from Galilee to the river Jordan so that John could baptize him.
John exclaimed, "Behold, the Lamb of God, who takes away the sin of the world!"
Hail Mary

John stopped Jesus, saying, "I need to be baptized by you, and you come to me?"
Hail Mary

But Jesus answered him, "Allow it now; for it is right to follow the will of God." Then John agreed.
Hail Mary

When Jesus was baptized and came up from the water, the heavens opened.
He saw the Spirit of God descending upon him like a dove.
Hail Mary

And lo, a voice from heaven said, "You are my beloved Son; on you my favor rests."
Hail Mary

Glory be to the Father, and to the Son, and to the Holy Spirit.
As it was in the beginning, is now, and ever shall be, world without end.
Amen.

DO WHATEVER HE TELLS YOU

MARRIAGE AT CANA
The Second Luminous Mystery

Our Father

One day, there was a marriage at Cana in Galilee, and the Mother of Jesus was there.
Jesus and his disciples were also invited to the wedding.
Hail Mary

When the wine ran out, the Mother of Jesus said to him, "They have no wine."
Hail Mary

Jesus said to her, "Oh, woman, what would you have me do? My hour has not yet come."
Hail Mary

His mother said to the servants, "Do whatever he tells you."
Hail Mary

Now six stone jars were standing there. Each one was able to hold twenty or thirty gallons.
Hail Mary

Jesus said to the servants, "Fill the jars with water."
Hail Mary

He then said, "Now draw some out and take it to the wine steward of the feast."
Hail Mary

The wine steward tasted the water that had now become wine,
and he did not know where it came from (though the servants knew).
Hail Mary

He called the bridegroom and said to him, "Every man serves the good wine first.
When men have drunk freely, then they pour the ordinary wine.
But you have kept the good wine until now."
Hail Mary

This, the first of his miracles, Jesus did at Cana in Galilee; and his disciples believed in him.
Hail Mary

Glory be to the Father, and to the Son, and to the Holy Spirit.
As it was in the beginning, is now, and ever shall be, world without end.
Amen.

Lord, I am not worthy
that Thou shouldst enter under my roof
but say only the word
and my soul shall be healed

Healing of the Sick
The Third Luminous Mystery

Our Father

Jesus traveled through cities and villages,
preaching and bringing the good news of the kingdom of God.
Hail Mary

He cured many people of diseases and plagues.
Hail Mary

He gave sight to those who were blind.
Hail Mary

The lame walked.
Hail Mary

Lepers were cleansed.
Hail Mary

The deaf were able to hear and the mute to speak.
Hail Mary

He cast out evil spirits.
Hail Mary

The dead he brought back to life.
Hail Mary

The poor had the good news preached to them.
Hail Mary

The crowds followed him wherever he went.
Jesus welcomed them and cured those who had need of healing.
Hail Mary

Glory be to the Father, and to the Son, and to the Holy Spirit.
As it was in the beginning, is now, and ever shall be, world without end.
Amen.

THE TRANSFIGURATION
The Fourth Luminous Mystery

Our Father

After preaching and healing in many villages,
Jesus took Peter, James, and John with him up on a high mountain to pray.
Hail Mary

As he was praying, his face shone like the sun and his clothing became white as light.
Hail Mary

Behold, Moses and Elijah appeared to them in glory, talking to Jesus.
Hail Mary

Peter said to Jesus, "Lord, it is well that we are here. If you wish,
I will make three tents, one for you and one each for Moses and Elijah."
Hail Mary

Suddenly, while he was still speaking, a bright cloud cast a shadow over them.
Hail Mary

From the cloud came a voice that said,
"This is my beloved Son, with whom I am well pleased. Listen to him."
Hail Mary

When they heard this, Peter, James, and John hid their faces and were very much afraid.
Hail Mary

But Jesus came and touched them saying, "Rise, and have no fear."
Hail Mary

When they lifted up their eyes, they saw no one but Jesus.
Hail Mary

As they were coming down the mountain, Jesus commanded them,
"Tell no one about the vision until the Son of Man is raised from the dead."
Hail Mary

Glory be to the Father, and to the Son, and to the Holy Spirit.
As it was in the beginning, is now, and ever shall be, world without end.
Amen.

The Ascension
The Second Glorious Mystery

Our Father

After he rose from the dead,
Jesus stayed with his disciples for forty days.
Hail Mary

He taught about the faith.
Hail Mary

He told them to love one another.
Hail Mary

He commanded Peter to guide his people, the church.
Hail Mary

He told the disciples to go out to teach and baptize people.
Hail Mary

He promised that he would send the Holy Spirit to help them.
Hail Mary

Finally it was time for Jesus to go home to his Father in heaven.
Hail Mary

He promised them, "I will be with you always, even to the end of time."
Hail Mary

As his followers watched Jesus go up into the sky, two angels said to them,
"One day Jesus will return, just as you saw him go up into the heavens."
Hail Mary

Upon witnessing Jesus' ascension, all the disciples were strengthened in their faith.
Hail Mary

Glory be to the Father, and to the Son, and to the Holy Spirit.
As it was in the beginning, is now, and ever shall be, world without end.
Amen.

PENTECOST

The Third Glorious Mystery

Our Father

After Jesus rose up to heaven,
the apostles and Mary waited and prayed together.
Hail Mary

Ten days later, a loud strong wind
suddenly blew through the upstairs room where they were sitting.
Hail Mary

Bright flames of fire settled above their heads.
Hail Mary

They felt the great power of the Holy Spirit filling their hearts with courage and love.
Hail Mary

The apostles were suddenly able to talk in many languages,
so that all people could understand what the Holy Spirit wanted them to say.
Hail Mary

Outside were people from every country.
They heard the sounds and came together to watch and listen.
Hail Mary

Peter explained to them that Jesus was a man sent by God to all people.
Hail Mary

He was nailed to a cross, died, and was buried.
But he rose again and was seen by the disciples.
Hail Mary

Now Jesus was in heaven with his Father.
Hail Mary

He sent the Holy Spirit to teach us what is true and good,
and to help us to love each other.
Hail Mary

*Glory be to the Father, and to the Son, and to the Holy Spirit.
As it was in the beginning, is now, and ever shall be, world without end.
Amen.*

THE ASSUMPTION
The Fourth Glorious Mystery

Our Father

Mary lived with the apostle John,
who took care of her as if she were his mother.
Mary treated John as her son.
Hail Mary

She encouraged all the apostles to work hard for Jesus.
Hail Mary

She prayed.
Hail Mary

She told children about Jesus.
Hail Mary

She visited sick people.
Hail Mary

She helped poor people.
Hail Mary

Mary wanted everyone to know God
and to be able to live in heaven with Jesus some day.
Hail Mary

Finally Mary's work on earth was finished
and Jesus wanted her to live forever with him.
Hail Mary

One day he sent angels to carry her gently up to him in heaven.
Hail Mary

Mary was very happy.
Hail Mary

Glory be to the Father, and to the Son, and to the Holy Spirit.
As it was in the beginning, is now, and ever shall be, world without end.
Amen.

CORONATION OF MARY
The Fifth Glorious Mystery

Our Father

Now Mary lives in heaven with God the Father,
Jesus the Son, and the Holy Spirit.
Hail Mary

She is the Queen of Heaven.
Hail Mary

She prays for us.
Hail Mary

She loves us.
Hail Mary

She wants each one of us to love Jesus with all our heart.
Hail Mary

She is our Heavenly Mother.
Hail Mary

She protects us.
Hail Mary

She comforts us when we are sad.
She wants us to be happy.
Hail Mary

She loves to talk with us
and hopes we will talk to her.
Hail Mary

Someday, when our work on earth is finished,
Mary wants us to live in heaven too.
Hail Mary

Glory be to the Father, and to the Son, and to the Holy Spirit.
As it was in the beginning, is now, and ever shall be, world without end.
Amen.

Author's Note

For centuries Christians have contemplated the "pictures" of the fifteen joyful, sorrowful, and glorious mysteries in the life of Jesus and Mary. Most recently, this "picture book" has expanded to include the five luminous mysteries, added by Pope John Paul II in 2002, which depict key events in the public life of Jesus. Like the stained glass windows or "picture catechisms" in medieval cathedrals that told the Gospel story for the illiterate believers, the rosary acts as a mini-catechism for people of all ages.

In fact, the rosary has deep scriptural and liturgical roots that go back to the time when monks recited all 150 Psalms together each week. Since this practice was limited to those who could read, 150 "paternosters" or Our Fathers came to be substituted for the Psalms and became a sort of "poor man's breviary." Starting in the twelfth century, when devotion to Jesus and Mary gained broad popularity, Hail Marys gradually replaced the Our Fathers. At this time the practice of stringing together rosary beads also emerged as a way to help people to meditate on the Lord with less distraction from counting. By the sixteenth century, our modern rosary had developed; fifteen mysteries became standard, as well as the additions of the Apostles' Creed, the Glory Be, and the second half of the Hail Mary: "Holy Mary, Mother of God, pray for us sinners, now and at the hour of our death."

Because the rosary is so intimately connected to Scripture, I was frequently inspired to intersperse passages adapted from the Gospels among the short meditations that precede the Hail Marys. The illustrations and the scriptural meditations thus work together, serving as mirrors that reflect and comment on one another. My hope is that these paintings will lead you on a journey of heartfelt communion with Jesus and Mary in the Gospels, so as to become ever more joyful children of our loving Father.